Children of the First People

Fresh Voices of Alaska's Native Kids

Profiles by Tricia Brown
Photographs by Roy Corral

ALASKA
NORTHWEST
BOOKS®

For Robert, John, Katiana, Selina, Andrea, Danny, Josh, and Tauni.

Acknowledgments:
Thank you Jennifer Newens, Olivia Ngai, Rachel Lopez Metzger, and Angela Zbornik of West Margin Press, and sincere thanks to our editor, Michelle McCann. We are grateful for your love and patience, Scooter Bentson, Perry Brown, and Kierra Morris. To the parents of the children and to others who supported us, you were invaluable. Thank you Tony Christianson and Jody Sanderson; Selina Tolson; Mary Beth Moss and Owen James; Don Starbard; Robert Starbard, Darlene See, Julie Jackson, and David See, Hoonah Indian Association; Jolene King; Bambi Jack; Sherry Mills; Jacob Pratt, Zach Inglesby, Ralph M. Watkins; Rosita Kaa háni Worl, Sealaska Heritage Institute and Sealaska Corporation; David Sparck; Sephora Lestenkoff; Chris Carmichael; Zachary Bastoky; Carla and Patrick Snow; Lance and Corina Kramer; Clement Richards, Sr.; Kristen Dau; Qaqutuk Janine Saito; Nick and Sara Tiedeman; Sheri Buretta, Chugach Alaska Corporation; Cybill and Nick Berestoff; Larry and Gail Evanoff; Doug Penn; Mike Hanley; Rebecca Gue; Dennis Fawcett; Rev. Larry Emery; Sue Scudero; Rev. Evon and Aquilina Bereskin; Bobbie Lekanoff; Okalena Patricia Lekanoff-Gregory; Ray Hudson and Rachel Mason; Ounalashka Corporation; Karen Cresh; Irene Adams; Joanna Hinderberger; Diana McCarty, William Flitt; Yaari Toolie; Alaska Native Heritage Center.

Text © 2019 by Tricia Brown
Photographs © 2019 by Roy Corral

Edited by Michelle McCann

Library of Congress Cataloging-in-Publication Data

Names: Brown, Tricia, author. | Corral, Roy, 1946- photographer.
Title: Children of the first people : fresh voices of Alaska's native kids / profiles by Tricia Brown ;
    photographs by Roy Corral.
Description: [Berkeley, CA] : West Margin Press, [2019]
Identifiers: LCCN 2018037986 (print) | LCCN 2019012306 (ebook) | ISBN 9781513261997 (ebook) |
    ISBN 9781513261973 (pbk.) | ISBN 9781513261980 (hardcover)
Subjects: LCSH: Indian children--Alaska--Juvenile literature. |
    Eskimo children--Alaska--Juvenile literature. | Eskimos--Juvenile literature.
Classification: LCC E78.A3 (ebook) | LCC E78.A3 B758 2019 (print) |
    DDC 979.8004/971--dc23
LC record available at https://lccn.loc.gov/2018037986

LSI2021

Published by Alaska Northwest Books
An imprint of West Margin Press

WEST
MARGIN
PRESS®

WestMarginPress.com

Proudly distributed by Ingram Publisher Services

WEST MARGIN PRESS
Publishing Director: Jennifer Newens
Marketing Manager: Angela Zbornik
Editor: Olivia Ngai
Design & Production: Rachel Lopez Metzger

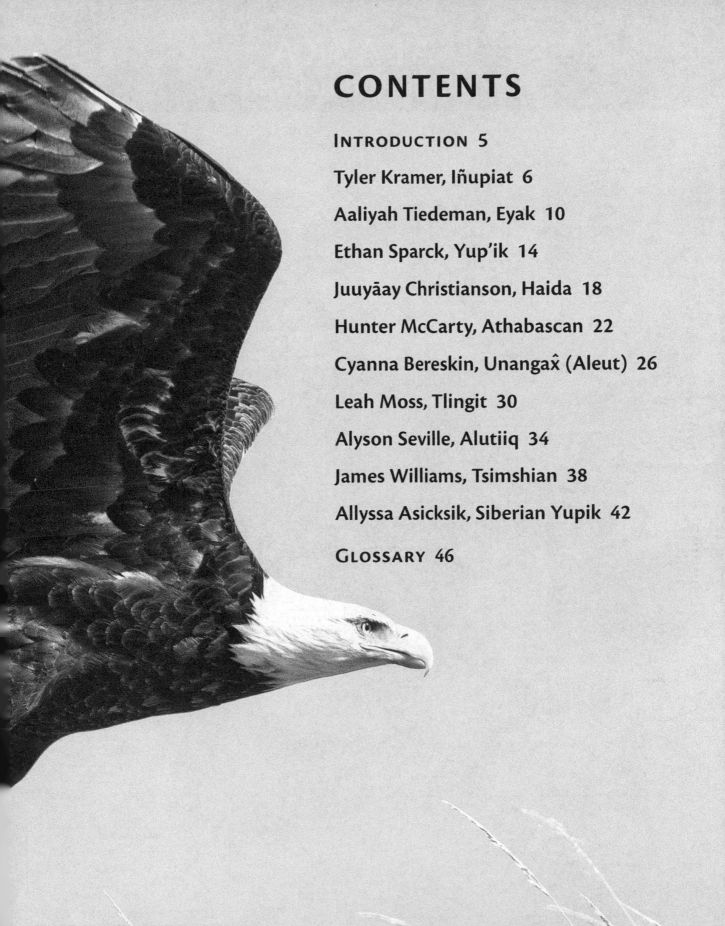

CONTENTS

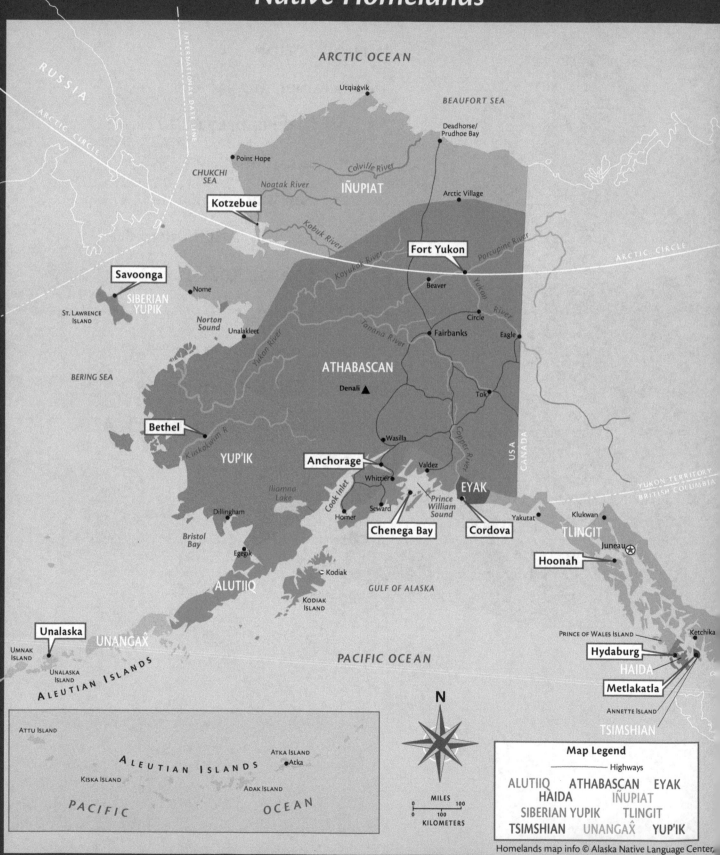

ALASKA
Native Homelands

ARCTIC OCEAN

BEAUFORT SEA

RUSSIA

ARCTIC CIRCLE

Utqiaġvik

Deadhorse/
Prudhoe Bay

Point Hope

CHUKCHI
SEA

Colville River

Noatak River

IÑUPIAT

Arctic Village

Kotzebue

Kobuk River

ARCTIC CIRCLE

Porcupine River

Fort Yukon

Koyukuk River

Beaver

Savoonga

Nome

SIBERIAN
YUPIK

Circle

Yukon River

River

St. Lawrence
Island

Norton
Sound

Unalakleet

Tanana River

Fairbanks

Eagle

BERING SEA

ATHABASCAN

Denali ▲

Tok

Bethel

Kuskokwim R.

YUP'IK

Wasilla

Copper River

USA
CANADA

YUKON TERRITORY
BRITISH COLUMBIA

Iliamna
Lake

Anchorage

Valdez

EYAK

Whittier

Dillingham

Cook Inlet

Prince
William
Sound

Yakutat

Klukwan

Bristol
Bay

Seward

Homer

Chenega Bay

Cordova

TLINGIT

Hoonah

Juneau ✪

Egegik

Kodiak

ALUTIIQ

Kodiak
Island

GULF OF ALASKA

PRINCE OF WALES ISLAND

Ketchika

Unalaska

UNANGAX̂

Umnak
Island

Unalaska
Island

ALEUTIAN ISLANDS

PACIFIC OCEAN

Hydaburg

HAIDA

Metlakatla

ANNETTE ISLAND

TSIMSHIAN

N

Attu Island

ALEUTIAN ISLANDS

Atka Island
Atka

Kiska Island

Adak Island

PACIFIC   OCEAN

MILES
0   100

0   100
KILOMETERS

Map Legend

—————— Highways

ALUTIIQ   ATHABASCAN   EYAK
HAIDA   IÑUPIAT
SIBERIAN YUPIK   TLINGIT
TSIMSHIAN   UNANGAX̂   YUP'IK

Homelands map info © Alaska Native Language Center,

Introduction: A New Generation Speaks

Long before the words of Alaska's first people were written in books, elders taught lessons by word of mouth and by example. Each new generation learned their culture's ways of living and how to thrive in their distant homes. Some lived in the rainforest; others in the Arctic. Some survived temperatures as cold as -50°F; others experienced a toasty 80°F. Their foods and housing and cultural memories were vastly different, but still, all were Alaskan.

Through the centuries and across the cultures, these important lessons have remained unchanged: show respect, take care of where you live, have patience, pray for guidance, share what you have, honor your elders, and more.

For today's Alaska Native children, culture classes are available in public and private school, yet everyday life is still their classroom. Haida master artisans show youngsters how to carve cedar totem poles, masks, and containers. Yup'iks who know which plants to pick for medicine invite children to come along and learn. Siberian Yupik apas (grandfathers) expertly read the weather and advise when it's safe to go out for bowhead whales. Tlingit uncles bring kids along as they hunt for deer or fish for salmon, sharing stories and cultural history while they train.

So have the children been paying attention? Are they remembering what they've been taught? Do they know what makes their particular culture unique? Many years ago, photographer Roy Corral and I asked those questions. To find answers, we set out to interview and photograph eight Alaska Native boys and girls for a book titled *Children of the Midnight Sun*. With help from village leaders and friends, we chose one child from each of the biggest

cultures and crisscrossed the state by small plane, ferry, and road. We rode on four-wheelers and behind snowmachines. We talked to families in every corner of Alaska.

After the book came out, we heard from readers in other states, saying things like, "That girl in the picture . . . she's just wearing jeans and a T-shirt like any other kid!" Yes, I'd answer, she really is just like any other kid. I explained that the children don't go around in their special regalia every day (those clothes are for cultural gatherings). And just like you, they struggle with homework and peer pressure. They play basketball, spend too much time gaming, and argue with their brothers. They imagine what they want to be someday. Sometimes they wish they could be somebody else.

On the other hand, where else can a kid say their ancestors have lived here for 10,000 years? And who can imagine tasting whale blubber, or drying kelp for a snack, or deftly tracking a moose, bear, caribou, rabbit, walrus, or seal? We discovered that Alaska Native kids are like all kids in some ways, but they don't realize how special they are. They seem to think, "Isn't everybody like me?"

Time has passed since that first book, and a new generation of Native kids is ready to speak. For this book, we decided to include all ten cultures, so we added the Siberian Yupik, Alutiiq, and Eyak people.

From the Southeast rainforest to the Yukon-Kuskokwim Delta tundra, to the reaches of the far north, traditional Native knowledge is still passed along. The children in this generation have been handed the precious gift of ancient heritage to carry into the future. We hope you enjoy meeting them.

IÑUPIAT

Tyler Kramer

Kotzebue

Ten-year-old Tyler Kramer is smiling as he begins his story, "Why Ground Squirrels Have Short Tails." He learned it from an elder just yesterday during Iñupiat [en-NEW-pee-at] Day at school, a chance for kids of all cultural backgrounds to learn about this region's first people.

"So, there was a Ground Squirrel out of his hole, and Raven was guarding it," Tyler begins. "And the Ground Squirrel said, 'If you would sing, then I'll dance to it.' And then the Ground Squirrel said, 'Now close your eyes . . .' And then, 'It would be better if you sang with your legs a little bit more open . . .' And Raven did that. And the Ground Squirrel ran through his legs to the hole. But the Raven grabbed its tail, and the tail came off!" Ancient stories from Alaska's far north can hold life lessons for listeners . . . and for ground squirrels too!

In many ways, every day is Iñupiat Day in Kotzebue, Tyler's hometown. It lies above the Arctic Circle at the tip of a peninsula. If Tyler could look over the curve of the ocean, he'd see Russia. Even on land, there's not much to block his view. "No trees," he says,

then reconsiders. "We have one, I think." Tyler's dad, Lance, laughs and adds, "Somebody planted it over by the base, an Air Force guy. We called it the Kotzebue National Forest. They had guys guarding it and everything."

Tyler's nickname is TyTy, and his Iñupiaq names are Alasuk, after a respected elder, and Tavra, for "all done" (which his mom declared after Tyler, her fifth child, was born). The entire family works together in a "subsistence lifestyle," what Alaskans call fishing and hunting for food, not for sport. The Kramers hunt caribou, moose, musk oxen, seals, and a variety of fish. They pick greens and berries, and collect seagull eggs just as the Iñupiats have done for countless centuries.

Tyler went on his first hunt when he was about six years old and last year caught his first caribou. He prefers the sea, however, especially spring seal hunting. "We don't get much whales here," he explains. In villages further north, other Iñupiats depend heavily on whales and walruses.

About 13,500 Iñupiats live on the North Slope, a region that sweeps from Norton Sound north and

Facing: Near midnight, Tyler is bathed in the last rays of a spring sun above the Arctic Circle. Above, left: Tyler learned how to bead from his aana (grandmother) and has several projects in progress. Right: Tyler is the youngest child in the Kramer family. From left is Cody, parents Corina and Lance, and Cassidy. Two other sisters are not pictured.

Above, left: In the centuries-old one-foot kick game, Tyler must jump, hit the ball with one foot, then land on the same foot. Right: Three "Eskimojis" pose on the high school gym floor.

eastward across the top of Alaska to the Canada border. Their traditional homeland experiences some of the harshest winters on the planet—the coldest cold, the longest dark. Only about 3,000 people speak Iñupiaq, their Native language, so teachers are working to improve that. Before a basketball game at the high school, where the Kotzebue Huskies host the Bethel Warriors, the Nome-Beltz Nanooks, or the Barrow Whalers, spectators start the evening with the Pledge of Allegiance . . . in Iñupiaq.

Adults want the next generation to know what it means to be Iñupiat, which means "The People" in English. Other Alaska Native cultures also refer to themselves, each in a unique language, as "The People" or "The Real People." Culture lessons aren't always taught at a desk, however. Everyday life is the classroom. Tyler learns from his dad, a local church pastor and set-net fisherman, who also traps for furs and tans hides to sell to skin-sewers. Tyler sets snares for foxes and rabbits. His aana (grandmother) teaches him how to sew mittens and parkas.

Out back a refrigerator has been converted into a smoker; a fish rack on the beach dries uġruk (bearded seal) meat in the spring, salmon and whitefish in the summer. The family shares their harvest with those who have less, especially with elders, an important aspect of Tyler's Iñupiaq heritage as well as his Christian faith.

Tyler has learned not only how to survive, but to thrive. He likes hamburgers and fries, but his favorite is Native food, like beluga muktuk (skin and blubber) with mustard, uġruk, and his mother's aqutuq [uh-qoo-tooq], Eskimo ice cream.

Not everything in this family is traditional, however. Tyler stars in his mom's social media videos and posts titled "The Life of Ty." Hundreds follow the adventures of this Eskimo boy living above the Arctic Circle.

This afternoon the Noatak team has flown in for a basketball game against Tyler's team, the "Eskimojis." As usual, boosters are selling candy, chips, and T-shirts with the Eskimoji logo—a smiling cartoon Eskimo face—and the question, "You cold, bro?" Tyler buys one.

In Alaska, it's okay to call these northernmost people "Eskimo," but some prefer just Iñupiat (for the group) or Iñupiaq (for a single person, language, or culture). In Canada's far north, however, the word Eskimo is insulting; they want to be called Inuit.

The people of the North Slope are crazy about basketball, but they also compete in ancient games that built muscle, endurance, and balance in hunters. At Christmas and New Year's, and during the Native Youth Olympics, everybody turns out to watch the one-foot kick, two-foot kick, stick pull, leg wrestling, ear pull, three-man carry, and knuckle hop. Almost all of them are pain-makers. Tyler once won the one-foot kick for his age, jumping up from a standing position and kicking one foot at a ball hanging 53 inches off the ground, then landing back on the same foot. That's more than four feet straight up.

Two summers ago, the family flew to Anchorage, piled into an RV, and drove "Outside" (what Alaskans call anyplace that's not Alaska). They roamed Canada and drove as far south as Texas. Tyler rode horses, walked among the tallest trees he'd ever seen, helped "peel" corn on the cob, and fished for trout in a campground pond until security cameras set off a squealing alarm. The owners asked him to stop—he'd caught too many fish.

On that trip, Tyler learned a lot about how other people live Outside. So when visitors from Idaho came up to Kotzebue, he was proud to teach them about his corner of the country . . . and do a little myth busting about the Iñupiat.

"They kept saying, 'I thought you guys lived in igloos, man!'" He laughs. "Um . . . no."

Top: A one-dog "team" named Jaxxi pulls her boy on the ice of the Chukchi Sea. Bottom: Ice-fishing is a favorite. Here, Tyler was hoping to catch a sheefish.

EYAK
Aaliyah Tiedeman
Cordova

Growing up in Cordova sets Aaliyah Tiedeman apart. First, by geography: Cordova is nestled at the base of Eyak Mountain on the Gulf of Alaska's Orca Inlet, surrounded by deep forests, migratory bird nesting areas, and sparkling water. The town is unreachable by road, so everyone comes and goes on planes or ferries (aka the Blue Canoes) of the Alaska Marine Highway.

Cordova was a mining boomtown that was officially organized in 1906. It was the end of the line for the Copper River & Northwestern Railway and a deep-water port for outgoing gold, silver, and copper. But centuries before the miners arrived, the Eyak [EE-yack] people lived in villages throughout this region. The place was and is bountiful—deer, fish, birds, and marine mammals for food and clothing; tall, thick trees for building homes and making art.

"There was no town," Aaliyah says. "This was just all trees. There were villages at Eyak Lake and other places. They used the Alaganik Slough to catch reds and silvers [salmon]. They just used all the natural resources. It's like a protected area now. You can't dig artifacts up."

The Eyaks are the fewest in number among all of Alaska's first people. They clashed with neighboring cultures to protect their hunting and fishing grounds. The Alutiiqs lived to the west, Athabascans to the north, and just beyond their eastern border, the mighty Tlingit. Eyak identity has survived through border disputes, a shrinking population, intermarriage, and the death of the last Eyak Native language speaker.

Nearly all of today's Eyaks are a blend of cultures, including Aaliyah. Her father, Nick, has Unangax̂ (Aleut), Tlingit, and Athabascan ancestors. Her mother is from the Upper Midwest and is part Chippewa Indian. Together, Aaliyah's parents teach their three daughters about living traditionally. They built their own cabin, fish and hunt for meat, and can fish. They also preserve berry and currant jams, jellies, and sauces to last until the next summer.

Each year, grades six and under participate in the

Facing: Aaliyah explores the small-boat harbor's protective breakwater along Orca Inlet. Above, left: Wearing traditional regalia, Aaliyah and other Eyak Dancers perform at the elementary school. Right: At Nuuciq Spirit Camp, she created a model based on her ancestors' kayaks.

As a reward for passing hunter safety class, Aaliyah's parents gave her a pink camo rifle.

school's Culture Week, where elders share language skills, traditional crafts, and old stories. In summers, Aaliyah's creative side blooms at Nuuciq [NEW-check] Spirit Camp.

"I'm really, really artistic," she says. "So I'll do a lot of skin-sewing. I've probably done about fifty things with skin-sewing and beading." Using furs of seals and sea otters, she has made wallets, pillows, and beautiful bags. At camp, her imagination casts back to the ancestors who walked this land and kayaked these waters. This year she made a model kayak.

"It's like the real thing," Aaliyah says. "That's exactly how they used to make it. Wood floats, obviously, but they needed to put a cover on it, and it was seal or sea-lion skin, but we used nylon."

Aaliyah's little hometown is a popular destination for tourists exploring its historic streets, the Pioneer Hall, the modern museum and library, and the Ilanka Cultural Center. They walk the fishing docks and enjoy seafood at local restaurants. There are no traffic lights here. The one flashing light is for the school zone.

Each February since 1961, itchy for spring, locals have hosted the Iceworm Festival. There are games, food, and a Miss Iceworm competition with a $2,500 scholarship prize. When she's old enough, Aaliyah hopes to enter. The parade finale features the town mascot, a blue iceworm, slithering down the street like a Chinese dragon, dozens of Cordovans walking inside.

"It has a huge face," Aaliyah says. "The person in the front, they have to work hard to keep the head up. And you kind of move it up and down.

"We do have iceworms here," she adds. "It's not a fairy tale." Aaliyah's right. Since the mysterious worms were discovered in 1887, scientists have learned they're only a few centimeters long, and that living on glacial ice suits them fine. If the temperature soars to 40°F, iceworms actually melt and die from the heat.

Most Cordova residents fish commercially or work in fish-processing plants. They were deeply affected when the *Exxon Valdez* tanker went aground in 1989 and brought disaster to their beloved Prince William Sound. The massive oil spill killed birds, marine mammals, fish, and other wildlife. For families that fished and gathered food for survival, it was devastating.

Aaliyah helps feed her family by dip-netting for salmon and deer hunting. Her .243 rifle, in pink camo, was a reward for passing the hunter safety course. She was thrilled to bring it on her first deer hunt.

"We were in a marshy area where the deer beds were," Aaliyah remembers. "We hiked up a couple hills; they weren't that steep. There were little hemlocks—the perfect tree for a gun positioner—so when you shot, your gun would be steady." Aaliyah and her father identified a small buck about sixty yards away. Her heart pounded as he coached her.

"I was shaky—I was like, 'Okay, calm down,'" Aaliyah says. "My dad was holding my shoulders and saying, 'Steady breathing.' Then I shot at it once, and it dropped. I was so proud of myself."

Afterward, Aaliyah followed the tradition of her people. "I thanked the animal, because I know my ancestors did it. They've given their life for you, for your family. That's the first thing we do. Once you drop the animal, you go down there and thank it."

In the spring, Aaliyah will fly to Anchorage for the Native Youth Olympics. She'll compete against girls from around the state in the Alaskan High Kick, which requires exceptional balance and strength.

The Wolverines basketball team must travel many miles by plane and ferry to compete.

She also loves basketball, both watching it and playing it. Plus there's listening to music while working out, spending time with friends, babysitting, and schoolwork. She's in advanced math and plans to study sports medicine someday.

As much as she has learned, Aaliyah still has many questions for her teachers. Not surprisingly for the future doctor, most are about health. "The medicine men . . . how did they figure out the people who were affected by this disease and what medicine they needed? And how did the first Eyak people learn how this plant was good [for medicine] and this plant wasn't?" Aaliyah is still learning.

YUP'IK
Ethan Sparck
Bethel

Some kids are playing on the swings and the slide; others are shooting baskets. The ball doesn't bounce on packed snow, but that's okay. Everybody knows you can't dribble, so they just pass and shoot.

Then lunchtime recess is over and it's time to head in to Bethel's Yup'ik [YOU-pick] immersion school called Ayaprun Elitnaurvik, meaning "School of the Bears." Inside, students are swishing around in unzipped coats and wet boots when the steady rhythm of a half-dozen drums begins. A *BOOM!* rolls out like a soft thunder clap. A pause, then another *BOOM!* Again and again, and getting louder.

Fifth-grader Ethan Sparck is among the drummers tapping taut fabric hoops with lightweight wands. Traditionally drums were made with seal or walrus skins, or the stomachs of caribou or beluga whales. But fabric is easier to stretch and won't dry and crack. An adult drummer begins singing in Yugtun [YOUX-toon], which these students speak and write as well as English. In the early grades, all lessons and conversations are in Yugtun. If you must speak in English, you must whisper.

Boys and girls toss lunch leftovers and wander over, one or two at a time, to find a space among dancers facing the singer-drummers. Boys throw down their coats to kneel on the soft bundle with heels under their bottoms. Their arms, hands, and heads begin to move in unison. The girls join them, standing in rows behind the boys, according to tradition. Their words and motions tell a true story that was worthy of a song.

"It was about a long time ago when people used powerful guns to go hunting out in the sea," Ethan explains. "One time an old man saw a seal. He took his gun and shot that seal, and when it came out of the water, he thought it was one seal, but he got two seals. One was hiding behind it."

Ethan translates the words of the song and explains its joyful ending. "The old man says, 'Holy cow!' when he sees that he got two seals, not just one." In an ancient culture that has survived through sharing food, a successful hunt means everything.

Ethan is as good at drumming and singing, speaking, and spelling Yugtun as he is at ice fishing, basketball, Wii Mini-Golf, salmonberry picking, or his latest hobby, knitting. It's a follow-up to the crochet skills he learned at age nine from his mother and grandmother. Ethan has made dishrags, hats, scarves, potholders . . . he loves it.

Later, at home, it's a typical afternoon. Ethan announces that there's no more room on his device to download even one more game, while his first-grade brother Adam pleads, "Can I play on your tablet?" Their creaky old Golden Lab, Jena, is also hungry for attention as the brothers huddle. She hobbles over and breathes on their laps.

Ethan's hometown of Bethel lies along the great

Facing: An accomplished drummer and dancer, Ethan plays a drum that once belonged to his grandfather, Harold Sparck.
Above: Bethel's welcoming sign highlights its connection to the famous dogsled race that begins and ends on the Kuskokwim River.

Kuskokwim River in southwestern Alaska, a nearly treeless region. Flying above it, the tundra seems to have more ponds, wetlands, and rivers than solid land. Most of the people who live there are Yup'ik, meaning "real person" in English.

Bethel is the go-to city for villagers along rivers in the Yukon–Kuskokwim (YK) Delta. It's where people fly for shopping, eating out, sports or cultural events, visiting, or traveling to and from Anchorage. Jets roar in and out of Bethel every day. From small, outlying villages, people come in propeller-driven planes that can land on short airstrips at villages like Akiachak, Eek, or Chevak, where Ethan's father, David, grew up. Ethan's grandfather was Harold Sparck, a white, Jewish man from the East Coast who long ago moved to Alaska and married a Cup'ik lady. He is remembered for fighting for Natives' rights.

As in most of Alaska, roads don't link the villages out here. To travel between them, you need a plane or boat. The exception is wintertime, when the Kuskokwim River freezes and becomes a snow-packed highway for trucks and fast-moving "snowmachines," as snowmobiles are called in Alaska. At spring "break-up" in May, the ice groans and grinds and finally breaks apart and floats out to sea—the Kuskokwim River comes alive again. All summer long, people go fishing, and barges deliver large freight, like trucks and building materials.

In the 1800s, when non-Native missionaries settled here along the river's cut bank, the Yup'iks advised against it. The newcomers didn't listen, however, so year after year the river chewed away at the bank until the Moravian missionaries had to cut their wooden houses in half, top to bottom, so they could drag the pieces away from the edge and then rejoin them. Now there's a seawall to protect the city.

Ethan's ancestors didn't live in wooden houses. They preferred sod homes partially dug into the

Below, left: Knitting is a new hobby. Right: Ethan, his brother Adam, and a cousin play among the aluminum fishing boats in Bethel's harbor.

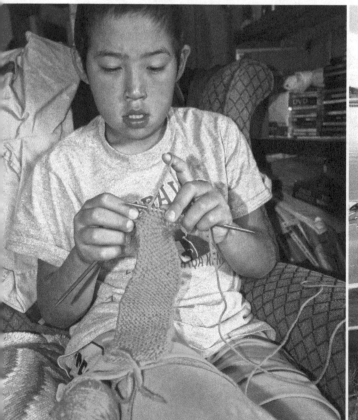

ground for natural insulation. They moved with the seasons, knowing where the fish and game would be plentiful, where the ducks and geese would pause in their migrations, where the berries would be at their peak. By autumn, they would have food safely stored, ready for the cold, dark curtain of winter to fall. Winter meant ice fishing and trapping for fur-bearing animals, then sewing tanned animal skins for clothing and shelter. A common phrase in the Yup'ik region was "always getting ready."

Just two generations ago, Ethan's Cup'ik grandmother was a little girl living in a traditional sod house and practicing the subsistence ways of her ancestors.

"Driftwood held up the ceiling," Ethan says. "They would weave grass to make their beds. They hunted lots of things like moose and seal, whales, rabbits, and other kinds of animals that have fur to keep them warm. And the women would sew their clothes."

These days the Real People live in modern homes and wear brand names or, like Ethan, jeans and a T-shirt. Sometimes an Adidas logo lies beneath a traditional fur parka. Shoppers can buy packaged chicken or hamburger, but most Yup'iks still prefer fresh fish and game they catch themselves. When he eats out, Ethan likes bacon-fried rice, steamer clams, or sushi. At home, he's big on soup: "We eat moose soup, seal soup, fish soup, bird soup, Canadian geese soup, swan soup, mallard soup . . ."

The Yup'ik people have lived a subsistence lifestyle for centuries and continue to do so still today. When the salmon are running, Ethan and his family take out their small aluminum boat and use a "drift net" to trap passing fish.

"We put the net over the edge of the back, then we motor away," he says. "Our net, it's not very long, so we'll catch maybe ten in each drift. One time we

The Sparck men—Ethan, Adam, and their father, David—step out on a windy day along the Kuskokwim.

caught sixty-two salmon in one day!" Some will be smoked, some frozen, some cooked fresh.

In the fall, temperatures drop and river ice builds, sometimes reaching three or four feet thick. On the radio, Bethel Search and Rescue advises when it's safe to drive on the ice. Then it's time to watch sled-dog racing or Ethan's favorite, manaqing, ice fishing for pike.

"We don't use a rod," Ethan says. "We use a stick with string and a hook on it. We make a hole with an auger, and then we unravel [the string] into the hole to the bottom." With pieces of blackfish as bait, Ethan will "jig" the line, jerking it slightly up and letting it fall. Later he will help cut and prepare their catch using his own ulaq, a curved knife.

One afternoon, Ethan and his fellow Bears are playing indoor basketball against boys from Bethel's other elementary school, the Cranes. They're nearly all friends or relatives and evenly matched. After the Bears beat the Cranes, Ethan grins, remembering a friend's pre-game trash talk. "He's a Crane, so he said to me, 'You run . . . we SOAR!'" On this day, however, it's Ethan's turn to soar.

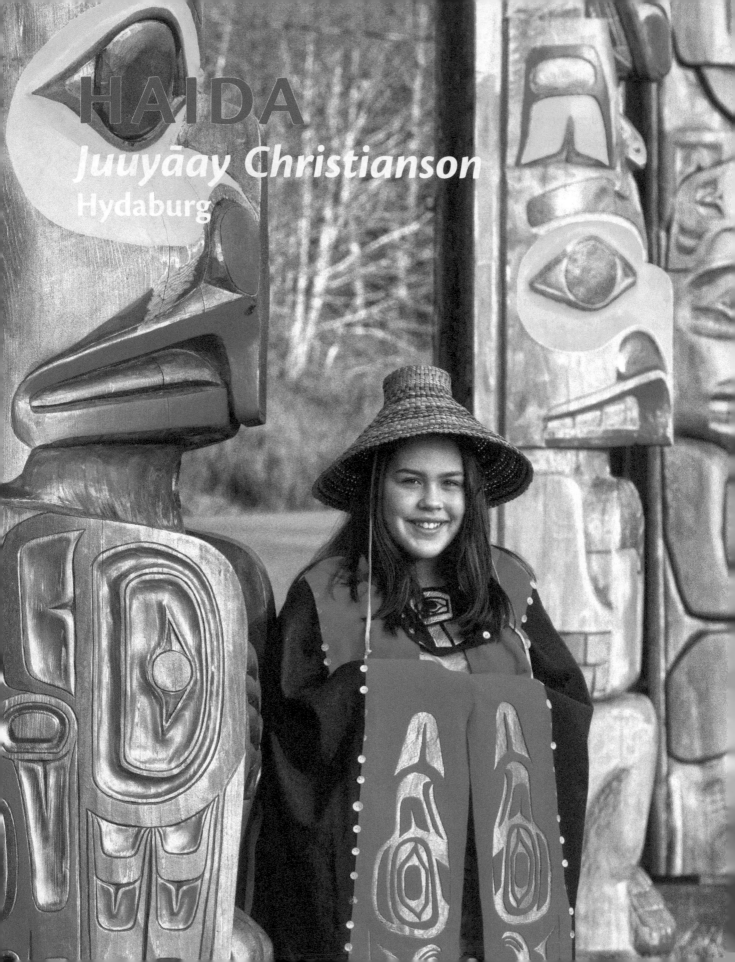

HAIDA

Juuyāay Christianson
Hydaburg

Juuyāay [JEW-eye] Christianson

plucks a deerskin drum off the living room wall to demonstrate how it's played. The surface is painted in the flattened, fantastic design of the Frog Clan crest, Juuyāay's people. The paint is worn where the wand has struck it again and again. Juuyāay waggles the drum stick with its "dance rattle" at the other end. A cluster of deer hooves makes a clacking sound.

Next she unfolds a long red-and-black cape edged with rows of flat white buttons. Called a "robe," it is designed to drape across the shoulders of a dancer, worn as he or she sways and steps to the drum beats and singing. The drum, dance rattle, and robe are part of ceremonial "regalia" that Haida [HI-duh] people wear for dances, clan celebrations called potlatches, or other Native festivals. Juuyāay's regalia items are family treasures, old and new, all handmade by loving aunties and grandmas.

"This one's kinda small," the twelve-year-old jokes as she pokes her head through a toddler-sized regalia piece. "I wore this when I was little." On the front is an image of a yellow sun with a Haida-style face. That's her: Juuyāay means "sun" in the Haida language. You might expect to see cultural treasures like these in a museum, but these pieces aren't behind glass. They're always in reach, brought to life at a touch.

To outsiders, the cultures of Southeast Alaska—the Haida, Tsimshian, and Tlingit people—look very similar. But each has its own unique regalia, totem carvings, legends, histories, and ways of living. Like other Native cultures, Haida traditions are centuries old, yet cannot be separated from everyday life. Dancing, drumming, singing, storytelling, and carving are not boxed up and set aside for special occasions. They are just normal—as normal as cheering for the Warriors in basketball regionals or taking selfies with friends.

Juuyāay's home is Hydaburg, on a sheltered shore of Prince of Wales Island. Their ancestors came from an island group called Haida Gwaii (or "Islands of the

Facing: Hydaburg Totem Park lies just outside Juuyāay's school. An Eagle, she wears her clan's design on her regalia.
Above: The village is reflected in the waters of Sukkwan Strait. Totem poles can be seen all over town.

People"), once known as the Queen Charlotte Islands, which lies just over the southern border in British Columbia. People have lived on Haida Gwaii for about thirteen centuries, but sometime in the late 1700s, a group of Juuyáay's ancestors canoed north and resettled on Prince of Wales. These Alaskans are called Kaigani [kigh-GONE-ee] Haida and about 400 live in Hydaburg today.

Forests of spruce, cedar, and hemlock edge Hydaburg, and the clear Hydaburg River rushes through the trees to enter the ocean beside the elaborately carved and painted long house. Kids like to swim and fish there at the mouth of the river. The town has no franchises: no fast food, fancy coffee, or big-box stores. Many people are subsistence hunters and fishers or are from commercial fishing families, and the ocean generously provides for all— salmon, halibut, clams, mussels, cockles, and crab. Hunters bring home deer meat. Planes and boats bring in the rest of the grocery list and other goods, from furniture to cars to building supplies. Here, your neighbor may have a totem pole standing in the front yard, and dinner may be venison and gravy over rice, or it may be frozen lasagna.

This Alaskan town lies within a rainforest and gets more than 100 inches of rain each year, but little snow. On this late January day, Juuyáay is walking around in a tie-dyed sweatshirt and flip flops while a thousand miles away in Fairbanks, other Alaskan kids are booted up for below-zero temperatures and many feet of snow.

The address for Juuyáay's school is Totem Pole Lane, a clue for what students see outside the windows. Rows of totem poles form a rectangle around their green space. As totems decay, as they often do in this rainforest climate, local artists carve them again, preserving their messages—honoring clans, remembering a great event, marking the death of a dear one. Juuyáay loves the totem poles and confesses that she loves learning too.

"Kids make it sound like school's so bad. It's not that bad," she says. "And when I come home, I'm still

Above, left: The Christianson-Sanderson family includes Juuyáay's dad Tony, mom Jody, and her sister, Ashley. Another sister is not pictured. Right: Out of school, cousins Ella Mooney and Juuyáay hang out in a local park.

learning things. I learn more about my culture every day. It's a fun place to live, actually."

At home, Juuyãay sticks her head in the refrigerator and announces, "The fridge contains literally nothing. I see some apples and oranges, some yogurt . . ." Later, during a walk around town, a truck stops and Juuyãay's dad jumps out for a hug. Tony Christianson is the mayor and an accomplished master carver who's always busy with something. But he pauses long enough to give Juuyãay some money. At a little store, Juuyãay buys Hot Pockets, Flaming Hot Cheetos, some beef jerky, and a Pepsi. *Thanks, Dad!*

"It's not always easy growing up where everybody knows you," Juuyãay says. "When I was younger, I'd get bullied: 'Oh, she's the mayor's daughter.' I didn't see it that way. I saw him as the guy I want to be someday when I grow up. My dad is my inspiration."

In Hydaburg, a child's identity begins not with their last name, but with the question "Raven or Eagle?" For many centuries, the Haidas' strict social laws have stated that every person belongs to one of these two groups, called "moieties." Each moiety is further divided into clans and sub-clans represented by crests of birds, fish, animals, insects, or reptiles—the figures you see on totem poles, traditional drums, dugout canoes, silver bracelets, and regalia. You can't join the bear clan just because you like bears—you have to be born into it.

Haida women, not men, hand down their clan identity to their children. So because Juuyãay's mother, Jody, is an Eagle, then Juuyãay and her siblings are also Eagle. Their sub-clan crests are Hummingbird and Frog, so those symbols are proudly displayed on their regalia and totem art. According to Haida rules, Juuyãay can only marry someone from the opposite

Living on an island means most families depend on the ocean for food, work, and play.

moiety. That means someday she will marry a Raven.

This evening at Juuyãay's home, the flat-screen TV stays dark after a delicious dinner of crab and deer meat with lots of side dishes. Family and friends pick up drums and rattles, and many (from toddlers to grandparents) dance to Haida songs. Mayor Tony is drumming and singing from his recliner. Auntie Selina is checking her phone messages with one hand, while her other hand keeps rhythm on her thigh. Juuyãay's two-year-old cousin is the star of the living room, beating his own tiny drum, cocking his head, crouching and bouncing. Híilangãay [he-lung-eye], which means "rolling thunder," is wearing a dinosaur T-shirt and Batman boots. He speaks Haida more often than English. With his cousin, the Sun, another generation prepares to take its place in Haida history.

ATHABASCAN
Hunter McCarty
Fort Yukon

Perched at the foot of a bed, Hunter McCarty and his cousin, Ben, are focused on a laugh-filled game of *Mario Kart*. Standing on each side of the older boys, two preschoolers jump and squeal as Hunter and Ben blast around the course, elbows tilting and fingers flying on the remotes. Behind him, Hunter's favorite books share a shelf with his collection of bear claws. And out in the living room, an NBA game is blaring as Hunter's mom, Diana, cleans up after a dinner of king salmon, rice, and salad.

Suddenly, the boys pour out of the bedroom and race to the pile of winter coats, boots, and snow pants by the door, noisily wriggle into them, and clunk outside. Several feet of snow are waiting.

"We get bored of playing video games," Hunter says. "Mostly I like to play outside, snowball fights and making snowmen . . . sometimes I go out there and just lay down. I'm used to the cold weather."

Hunter lives in Fort Yukon—near where the Yukon River crosses the Arctic Circle—about 145 air miles north of Fairbanks. It's -2°F on this first day of spring. In winter, temperatures can hang out at -30°F or even -40°F, and woodstove smoke settles in a flat cloud over the village of 600 people. Right now, the surface of the wide, frozen Yukon River is a mess of buckled ice and overflow, where water has squeezed up through cracks. It's too dangerous to drive trucks or snowmachines, or even to walk on the river. In late March, winter will loosen its grip, and long days of sunshine will warm Fort Yukon during Spring Carnival, with its sled-dog races, Jig Dance, sleeping bag races, nail-driving contest, and a huge banquet. Hunter's sister is one of the organizers.

Hunter is an Athabascan from the Gwich'in-speaking region and has more relatives downriver among the Koyukon speakers. Gwich'in means "people of the caribou," and they speak one of eleven distinct Athabascan languages. Among all Alaska Native groups, there are more Athabascans than any other. Their traditional homeland covers the state's Interior and beyond, even crossing over into Canada's Yukon Territory. Of course, boundary lines drawn on maps hundreds of years ago meant nothing to Hunter's ancestors, nor to the four-legged animals, birds, and

Facing: Each snowy spring weekend, Fort Yukon hosts "Dog Derbies," or short sled-dog races, near town. Hunter's warm hat is made of marten fur. Above, left: Hunter owns an impressive collection of bear claws. Right: Tyler and family pile on the couch together: mom Diana, brother Tyler, and nephews Cody and Hammel.

Above, left: Practicing is fun when you love the guitar as much as Hunter does. Right: Even though he's young, Hunter has learned how to safely handle a firearm, a necessary skill he must acquire before he could go on his first hunt. Here, Hunter and his brother, Tyler, are looking for snowshoe hares—rabbits with extra-large hind feet.

fish that they depended on for food and clothing.

Hunter is the youngest of four children, born more than eleven years after the others. In a way, he's like an only child. His brother, Tyler, and sister, Corrina, bring him on their hunting trips and on sled-dog runs. This fall Hunter joined his uncles, cousins, and siblings to boat and camp on the Black River during his first moose hunt.

"I think we spotted at least twelve moose," Hunter says. "You can't kill a female, and you can't kill a young one, because they might go extinct." Rabbits, Hunter says, are his favorite catch. He and Tyler have gotten several this winter. "We bring them home for food. They're really good. Mom cooks them . . . she fries them," he says, joking, "Tastes like chicken!"

Bears routinely wander into Fort Yukon, and parents always look around before sending children or pets outside. Hunter knows his bear safety: "Let's say if you see a bear," he says, "always think, they're more scared of you than you are of them."

Hunter's Athabascan ancestors were mobile people who traveled in bands and depended on each other and the natural world around them for survival. They used caribou and moose hides to make clothes, blankets, and boots. Beaver skins made mittens. Their temporary homes were dome-like tents of skins over bowed tree limbs. Then in 1847, a British-Canadian man set up a trading post here. Some Gwich'ins began settling nearby for trade, and soon living in one place became normal. Still, each summer families left for "fish camp" on the river, where they cut, then smoked or dried their catch. That tradition continues today. The sight of an Athabascan fish wheel lazily turning in the river current is common. Salmon swim into giant baskets that lift them out of the water and gravity drops them into a container.

Those long-ago British and American traders left traces of their cultures. The tradition of Athabascan fiddling began with those non-Native travelers. Today no Fort Yukon potlatch, or community gathering, is complete without square dancing, waltzing, or jigging to fiddle and guitar music. Athabascan skin-sewers also adopted beautiful floral patterns from French-Canadian designs. Women still use those patterns for beading flowers and leaves onto caribou or moose hide jackets, vests, and slippers. Hunter's mother is a skilled beader.

Fort Yukon might not even be here today if one incredible plan had succeeded. As early as 1954, before Alaska statehood, developers and politicians were studying ways to build a hydroelectric dam on the Yukon River. If the dam had been built, nine Alaskan villages—including Hunter's—would have been under water in the resulting 270-mile-long lake. It would have wiped out homes and destroyed habitat for uncountable salmon, bears, moose, caribou, sheep, and waterfowl in the Yukon Flats region. The potential disaster was averted in June 1967, when the U.S. Secretary of the Interior decided against the dam.

Hunter goes to Fort Yukon Elementary, home of the Eagles, where the youngest grades share class-rooms and the older grades have their own. Language arts and science are his favorite subjects. He likes learning words in the Gwich'in language too. That's good news to elder William Flitt, who grew up here, learning from generations before him, including his grandmother, Fannie William, who lived to be 126. Flitt now teaches the younger generation by "talking, talking, talking" about survival and how to live a good life, whether it's in Fort Yukon or another Gwich'in village. Each one is unique, yet connected.

"There's lots of different type of people in here, but we could hear each other, our language," Flitt says. "Some of them are different, like our tradition is king salmon and moose and all that, and way up in Arctic Village, that's a caribou area. They're caribou people. We grow up lots of different way. But we hear each other. We work together. It's good people."

Hunter knows the feeling of community, of ancestry, especially when he's out on the land.

"Yeah. It's hard to explain," he says. "I just feel like I . . . like someone has been here before, someone related to me."

Hunter's responsibilities at home include carrying wood for his mom. Their woodstove helps keep their home warm in winter.

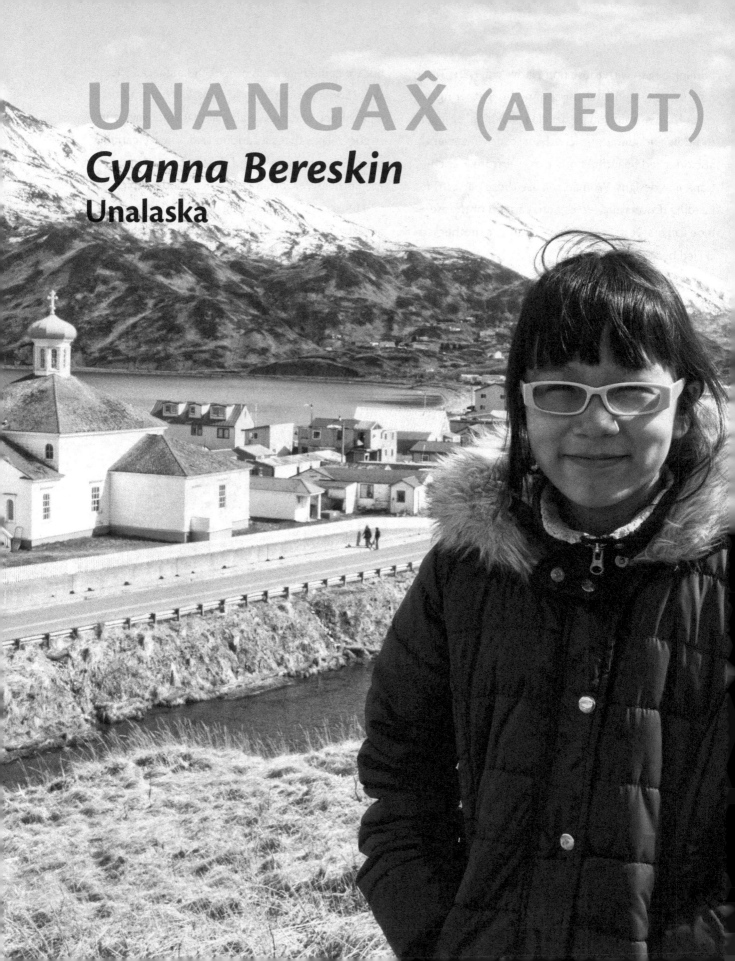

UNANGAX̂ (ALEUT)

Cyanna Bereskin
Unalaska

It's a blustery night on Unalaska Island, and eleven-year-old Cyanna Bereskin and her sister Nellie are walking to Easter service at 11:30 p.m. The girls wear frilly dresses under warm coats and stay on the sidewalk to keep their boots nice. They don't have far to walk because they live nearby—their dad is the Russian Orthodox priest at the historic Holy Ascension Cathedral.

Cyanna calls herself a tomboy and isn't crazy about the clothes she's wearing. "I'm not that girly," she says. "I don't like puffy dresses." But Cyanna does love family and holiday traditions. She helped boil Easter eggs to hand out at 3:00 a.m., when the service ends. And then comes the big family breakfast, getting out of that girly dress, and sleeping in. Cyanna also loves chasing her energetic puppy, learning the trombone, and laughing with Nellie, especially when they play their made-up game called "Little Guy."

"We make little houses out of books." Cyanna smiles as she explains. "Sometimes we use Barbie clothes, but we don't even play with Barbie. We put the clothes on our fingers, little pants and dresses."

She straightens her fingers and "walks" along her leg to demonstrate Little Guys walking around their little city. Stacks of old VHS tapes make good houses too.

The Bereskin house overlooks Iliuliuk Bay on this craggy, mountainous island, one of dozens in the Aleutian Island chain reaching across the Pacific Ocean for a thousand miles. The islands are dotted with the volcanoes (some still active!). Fewer than 5,000 people live in Cyanna's town, also named Unalaska, where there's lots of wind, but few trees. A bridge leads to Amaknak Island and the airport, hotel, museums, and grocery store. Reality TV fans can drive further out to Dutch Harbor and take pictures of the huge crabbing boats featured on *Deadliest Catch*. (Cyanna prefers the cartoon channel.)

But the island's most photographed attraction is her church, a National Historic Landmark from 1894 with tall Russian crosses atop onion-shaped domes. Bald eagles often perch up there, feathers fluffing in the strong winds. During the Christmas Bird Count, volunteers estimated 600-plus eagles around Unalaska.

When Cyanna enters church on Easter, it is dark.

Facing: Cyanna's hometown and her island are both named Unalaska. Above, left: Russian Orthodox Easter here includes boiling eggs and giving them away after the church service. Right: Bundled up against the wind, Father Evon Bereskin and daughters Nellie and Cyanna stroll past the graves of ancestors.

Above, left: Cyanna and Nellie share ownership of their puppy. Right: Bald eagles seem to pose for tourists who arrive here to photograph Unalaska's historic places and its migratory birds.

The little choir uses a single penlight to read their song sheets. Cyanna doesn't sing but stands among them with her mom, Aquilina. A capella songs in English and Slavonic, the language of Russian worship, echo beautifully. Religious icons and centuries-old paintings glow as the people stand, men on the right and women on the left, throughout the long service.

"If we get tired, we lay down on our coats," Cyanna says, speaking for the children, and Nellie does rest by her mother's feet that night.

Cyanna's mom is Yup'ik, while her dad is Aleut [al-ee-OOT], a name given to his ancestors by Russians who believed it meant "island" in the local language. Calling someone "Aleut" is fine, but many prefer their original name, Unangax̂ [ooh-NAHN-gach], meaning "people." They've lived on these islands at least 10,000 years, too far back to count the generations. The Unangax̂ first saw foreign explorers and hunters in the mid-1700s, a time that's called "contact."

"The Aleuts used to live in hills called barabaras [buh-RA-buh-RAs]," Cyanna says. The semi-underground homes were supported with driftwood in walls and ceilings. "And they made stuff out of weaving, like baskets."

Until contact, the people had known little change. They built skin-covered kayaks to hunt marine mammals for food and clothing. They hunted waterfowl, collected eggs, and gathered food from tide pools. They carved atlatls [AT-ul-AT-uls] to increase the speed and accuracy of their spears. They tattooed their bodies—even their faces—using bone needles and sinew thread to sew soot under their skin.

Because the Unangax̂ were the first of Alaska's Native cultures to clash with foreigners, they may have lost the most. Before contact, as many as 12,000 people lived in small villages along the chain. When Russians discovered the value of sea otter furs, they forced Native men to hunt for them. Many Natives died from starvation, battle, and disease. By 1800, only about 2,500 Unangax̂ remained, most with Russian surnames and a new religion. In time, their dances, language, and songs were nearly forgotten.

Cyanna's last name is Russian. And her first name honors a fifteenth-century Orthodox nun. But she's also very interested in her Native heritage. She and other kids learn about their ancient history at culture camps and in Unangax̂ class.

"At camp, I weaved," Cyanna says. "I made a doll too. They already made the body, and we sewed the clothes and put on the hair out of fur and drew the face." Cyanna even added facial tattoos to her doll. The fifth-grader also competes in Native Youth Olympics. Her best events are the Alaskan High Kick and the Scissor Broad Jump, which is like a long jump, but one leg must cross behind the other once during the run-up.

Cyanna's people survived those early foreign invasions by blending Russian culture in with their Native heritage. But a later foreign invasion was more devastating. During World War II, the Japanese dropped bombs on Unalaska and Amaknak in repeated attacks that began on June 3, 1942. Enemy soldiers also invaded Attu Island and captured a group of U.S. citizens—including Unangax̂ children—and took them to Japan as prisoners of war.

The U.S. government then sent a military ship to collect the rest of the Unangax̂ along the Aleutian Chain and the Pribilof Islands and took them to two camps in Southeast Alaska, where they spent the remaining war years living in crowded, unclean conditions, far from their homes. Many died there. After the war, survivors were returned to Unalaska, but for some, their remote villages had been destroyed in the fighting. The story isn't found in most schoolbooks. Reminders from the war are everywhere—from foxhole and trench scars on hillsides to rusting remains of gun turrets and ammunition storage.

"What happened, happened," says Cyanna's dad, Father Evon. "In their mind, they were trying to protect us." He's sad that the Unangax̂ experience is rarely taught outside of the Aleutians.

As for Cyanna, she continues to gather the many pieces of her heritage puzzle. In late July, she'll attend Camp Qungaayux̂ [COO-naye-ach] at Humpy Cove when pink salmon, or "humpbacks," are running. Kids will learn how to net fish, mend nets, and weave. They'll make Aleut visors, preserve and prepare seal, fish, and edible plants, and practice dancing, singing, and the words of their first language, Unangam Tunuu.

There's a note of pride in Cyanna's voice when she says, "I'm half-Yup'ik, half-Aleut . . . mostly English."

A day after Easter, Cyanna's family gathers for a portrait. At left are her Yup'ik grandparents, who were visiting from Kwethluk, Alaska. At right are the Bereskin sisters and their parents, Aquilina and Father Evon.

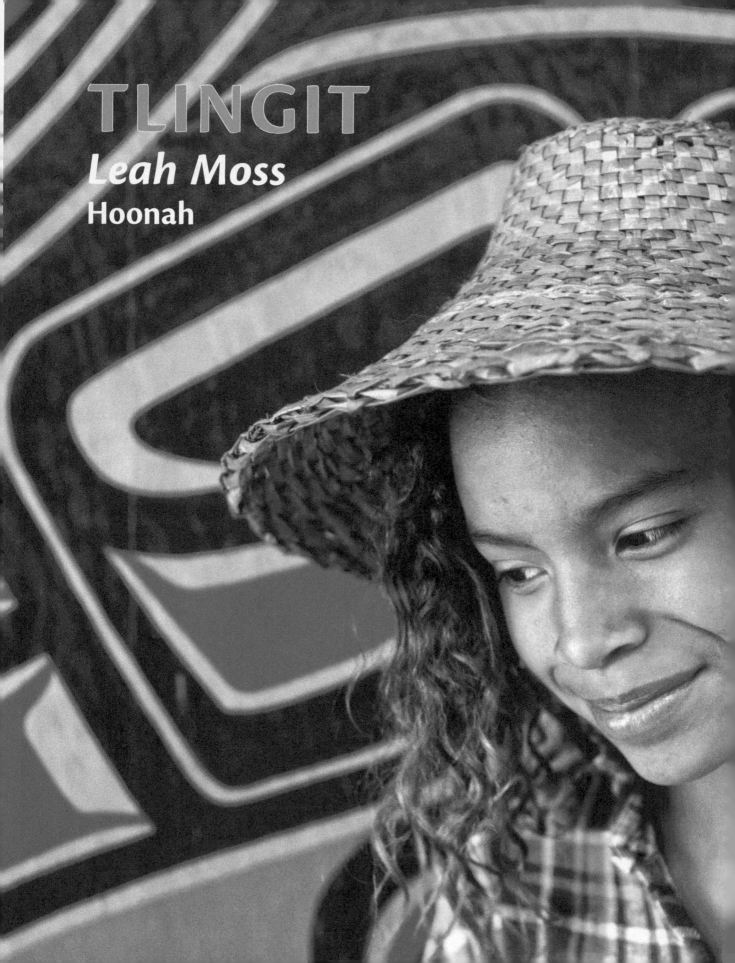

TLINGIT

Leah Moss

Hoonah

Leah Moss unzips her snack baggie.

It's snowy outside, but the scent from the bag is salty and summery, and far healthier than chips. It's dried seaweed and Leah loves it. She and her friend dip in, then return to building their papier-mâché likeness of the Mayan temple known as Xunantunich in Belize. Leah frets about how to make tiny trees. "What could we use?" she asks her mom.

Leah's home is at least two plane rides (or a plane and a ferry ride) away from where most Alaskans live. Still, with 750 residents, more than half of them Alaska Natives, Hoonah has the largest population of Tlingit [KLINK-it] people in the state. The Tlingit homeland once included all of "Southeast," the temperate rainforest along the southeastern coast, and extended into Canada. That was before non-Natives discovered its furs, gold, salmon, timber, and more. Before foreigners explored and claimed and named its parts. Today most of Southeast is federally protected in the Tongass National Forest or Glacier Bay National Park and Preserve, which together cover more than 20 million acres.

Leah lives in a roomy, woodstove-heated house. She gets good grades in Tlingit language class, and in basketball she's a serious competitor. Most of all, she loves singing and drumming. This summer she'll join the local dance group during "Celebration," a four-day gathering of Tlingit, Haida, and Tsimshian people in Juneau. Leah laughs at Celebration videos from when she was two, when she stole the show, fearlessly bobbing and weaving to ancestral songs.

Extended family is everywhere. Like Leah, they each know how they fit in their culture: moiety, clan, and clan house groups. For millennia, these social groupings have governed how Tlingit identify who they are and what is expected of them. Hoonah's four primary clans are Chookaneidí, T'akdeintaan (Leah's clan), Wooshkeetaan, and Kaagwaantaan.

"Wanna see my paddle?" asks Leah, "I made this with my daddy." She holds up a carved canoe paddle painted with a Seagull, the crest of her clan house, similar to the sub-clan in another culture. Moiety and clan membership is passed through the Tlingit mother's side. If your mother's moiety is Eagle, you are

Facing: Leah Moss's traditional regalia includes a hat woven from split-and-dried cedar bark strips. Above, left: Leah and a friend join her dad on a walk through their small town, where everybody knows each other. Right: In a traditional Tlingit dugout canoe, Leah and others hold their paddles upright, showing friendship.

Above, left: With the Ch'eet Screen behind them, Owen James and daughter Leah sing a Tlingit "entrance song" in the Yaakw Kahidi canoe house and shed. Right: With lots of practice, Leah has mastered both front and back flips on her trampoline.

an Eagle. Children learn clan stories, traditions, and duties from their mom's brother, another Eagle.

At school, Leah finds a seat in Tlingit language class, where signs all over the room attach Native words to objects or photos. It's nearly Valentine's Day, so today is about love. I likoodzí [Ee-tla-COOT-zee] means "You are awesome (or amazing, wonderful)." Ixsixán [Eex-si-xon] means "I love you."

"It's kinda hard pronouncing the underlined x's and the pinched k's," Leah says. "The underlined x's are like, clearing your throat, and the k's are like KA, real sharp. It doesn't come easily."

Leah's Tlingit name, Kooxwuduya [Koox-woo-doo-yuh], means "something brought back to its place of origin." Like many Alaska Native women, Leah's birth mother traveled to Anchorage to have her baby at the Alaska Native Medical Center. But as an infant, Leah came back to Hoonah when tribal leaders approved Mary Beth as Leah's adoptive mother. Mary Beth is

not Native, but as a cultural anthropologist for the National Park Service, she teaches tourists about the Tlingit culture. Leah's adoptive father is a Tlingit from Kake, Alaska, a respected carver and culture-bearer known as "Papa Owen" to the kids he teaches.

For Leah and her people, Hoonah is home. And yet it isn't their only home. For centuries, their ancestors lived at the foot of a glacier about 30 miles north, near what is now called Glacier Bay. There they thrived on seals, deer, and salmon; cockles and mussels; berries and seaweed. They gazed at mountaintops draped with ice and snow. The Tlingit carved cedar canoes and paddles and mastered the dangerous currents between islands. They made art, raised families, and passed on their histories and legends by speaking them, generation to generation.

"What do you suppose it would have been like, living that close to a glacier?" Mary Beth asks Leah, who answers, "Cool." She doesn't mean "cool" as in "hip"—she means cold. Winds off the glacier would have chilled the village, and the nearness of an advancing river of ice would have been ominous.

One terrifying day, the glacier broke loose and ice roared toward the village. It moved, the story says, "as fast as a running dog." The people fled before their village was destroyed and narrowly escaped in dugout canoes, leaving ripples of sorrow in their wake. They explored and finally chose the site of today's Hoonah, or Xunaa, which means "protected from the north wind." Anthropologists like Leah's mom listened to old recordings, interviewed elders, and talked to scientists who studied tree rings to estimate historical dates. They believe Hoonah was settled around 1754 ... yet home for these Tlingit will always lie in Glacier Bay.

One foggy morning in late August 2016, children wearing beautiful red-and-black regalia waited on Bartlett Cove of Glacier Bay as three hand-carved canoes approached the newly built tribal house, Xunaa Shuká Hít, or "Ancestors' House." The paddlers, also in traditional clothing, paused with their paddles upright, the sign of peace. From the canoes, elders called out centuries-old Tlingit greetings and asked permission to land. Leading the crowd on shore, Leah welcomed them in Tlingit.

On that remarkable day, Leah's people regained a sliver of their long-ago loss and celebrated in the grandly carved Ancestors' House. Leah's father, Owen, was among three craftsmen who spent years on the painted carvings.

After school, Leah leads the way to her dad's carving shed (after a brief stop to buy candy). The scent of fresh cedar fills the shed, and Owen is bent over a totem pole on supports. Curls of cedar

They may look like rocks, but black oystercatcher eggs are collected for food. Because the eggs are camouflaged among beach rocks, predators often overlook them.

shavings lie underfoot. While Leah listens, Owen explains the figures and what they mean: the four primary Huna clans, the glacier's face, and the woman who sacrificed herself when the glacier overran the winter village. Chains are for the period when the Tlingit were kept from their homeland, after the U.S. government took it for public parkland. Healing a century of hard feelings, tribal leaders and park leaders made peace with the building of the Ancestors' House. Oral history has been recorded in this wood.

One day this pole will be raised outside the Ancestors' House in Glacier Bay. And years from now the elements will weather Owen's art, but the history will not fade. And the story of the children who reclaimed their heritage, led by Leah, will live on.

ALUTIIQ

Alyson Seville

Chenega Bay

The mail plane has come and gone

in Chenega [chuh-NEE-guh] Bay, leaving shipping boxes that crowd Alyson Seville's living room. They're jammed with good things to eat: crackers, mac and cheese, cereal, rice, chips, cookies, and more. Mail-order groceries are a way of life in Chenega Bay, where about seventy-five people live and where going grocery shopping often means salmon fishing or hunting for deer, seal, geese, or ducks.

The food they order by mail can't be fresh or frozen, so there's no meat, milk, or ice cream, which might melt or spoil during a flight delay. Still, mail plane day feels like Christmas. Excited, ten-year-old Alyson and her little sisters are bent over, almost falling into the boxes as they pull out their favorites. For Alyson, it's a brick of cheddar cheese.

Alyson is an Alutiiq [ah-LOO-tick] girl living in Chenega Bay, her stepdad's home village. Chenega means "beneath the mountain" in Sugt'stun [SOOK-stoon]. Her mom is from Nanwalek, another Alutiiq coastal village. Homeland for their people, who are also known as Sugpiaq [SUG-pea-ak], stretches from the Alaska Peninsula eastward across the islands of Kodiak, part of the Kenai Peninsula, and along the coasts and islands of Prince William Sound. Alyson's ancestors were expert sailors who made kayaks, skin-covered boats, to hunt for sea mammals. Today the small-boat harbor holds commercial fishing boats and smaller aluminum skiffs, including one that belongs to her family.

Alyson's parents and grandparents still depend on the ocean and the land for meat and fish. Her stepdad fills the freezer with duck and deer meat, but her favorite food is "ba-sketti," the way her mom makes it. She's learning how to hunt too.

"One time I did geese hunting. I didn't get any, but I was so close," she says. "And I went seal hunting."

Beginning in the mid-1700s, Russians explored, traded, and married into this culture and others, so many villagers inherited Russian-sounding surnames. Through the work of long-ago Russian Orthodox missionaries, communities like this one are proud of their lovely blue-domed churches. Here, the Nativity of the Thetokas church is known for its

Facing: Alyson's family is from two different Alutiiq villages. In her dad's home village of Nanwalek, she faces Kachemak Bay. Her other home is Chenega Bay on Prince William Sound. Above, left: The inside of her church displays the skills of many artists. Right: As the oldest child, Alyson gets to help with baking (and babysitting her three little sisters!).

Above, left: Where Alyson lives, the ocean doesn't freeze. Tall mountains skirt the edges of the bay. Right: On January 7, Russian Christmas, Alyson joins her mom, Cybill Berestoff, in the "Starring" holiday tradition of walking, singing, and snacking from house to house.

craftsmanship, its mosaic floor, and elegant icons, and murals of Jesus and the Alaskan saints.

Chenega Bay has a school, an airport, a medical clinic, and a ferry dock for the Alaska Marine Highway. Unless you fly here in a small plane, boats are the only way in or out. Each summer from mid-May to mid-September, passengers can ride the ferry for four and a half hours to reach Whittier, which is on Alaska's road system. Sailing to Kodiak Island takes fourteen hours.

Alyson's favorite time of year is summer, especially when the weekly ferry stops here. The on-board restaurant is like a floating diner on their doorstep. She and her friends tear down to the dock for a tasty treat while passengers and freight come and go.

"We go on the boat, and we get soda and stuff like that, and milk," Alyson says, "and we get chicken strips and cheeseburgers. Sometimes when we're down there, we jump off the dock, and sometimes I

go fishing. It's really cold when you first jump in."

Alyson is the only fourth-grader at Chenega Bay School. Having the entire grade all to herself is "a little weird," she says, but sharing a classroom with older grades leads to faster learning. She loves school and even plays School with her little sisters, teaching them with flash cards and singing her ABCs. Someday she hopes to be a cook, an artist, and a singer.

"I like math," Alyson says. "And I like to write and read." On this winter day, a traveling science teacher has arrived to lead students in building shoe-sized motorized cars to race. Alyson crouches over her invention, trying different wheels to improve its performance. Eventually it flies across the gym floor.

After school, Alyson leads a tour of Chenega Bay while Posey, her white kitty, daintily follows behind in the snow. Posey's little nose and ears are pink from cold, but she's a snow cat, never heading home, but always following her girl. Even during a warm-up inside the church, Alyson looks up to see Posey nosing the glass door, looking for her. *Sorry, no cats in church.*

For close to ten centuries, Alyson's ancestors lived on Chenega Island with their backs to the soaring, forested mountains and their faces to the cobalt blue of Prince William Sound. Then, on March 27, 1964, a 9.2-magnitude earthquake rocked Alaska. After the earthquake, a tsunami, or tidal wave, blasted the coast. In Kodiak, huge fishing boats were lifted out of the harbor and thrown down city streets. The massive wave flattened Valdez. Many died. But no place suffered greater than Chenega Bay, where more than a third of the residents were killed and their village wiped out.

Those who survived the disaster moved to other towns. In 1984, after much planning, some of the survivors came together to build a new village on ancestral land on Evans Island, the current location. The new Chenega Bay faced danger again just a few years later. On March 24, 1989, an oil tanker called the *Exxon Valdez* went aground and spilled 10.8 million gallons of crude oil into Prince William Sound. Millions of birds, fish, and sea mammals died, and the Native people of the region lost their main food resources. Decades later, oil from that spill can still be found on nearby beaches. Some creatures have bounced back, like sea otters and humpback whales; others, like herring, have not.

Sometimes when Alyson is down by the ferry dock, she listens for the singing of those humpback whales as they migrate past her village. Their sound is hard to describe, for scientists as much as for fourth-grade girls who are used to it.

"They make that humming kind of sound," Alyson says. "Say like you're singing to a baby, but not actually singing to it. You add all that together."

Top: Plastic sleds move extra fast when the snow is coated with ice. Bottom: In January, the sun sets after only six hours of moving just above the horizon.

TSIMSHIAN
James Williams
Metlakatla

My name is James. My crest is Killerwhale.
I am from Metlakatla.
I am from the House of the Blue-Billed Duck.

James Williams first speaks the words in Sm'algyax, the language of the Ts'msyen, or Tsimshian [sim-she-ANN] people. Quickly he follows with the English translation. For this twelve-year-old boy from Annette Island, the words are the roadmap of his identity.

"In the Tsimshian culture, there are four main clans: Eagle, Raven, Wolf, and Killerwhale," James explains. "I am Killerwhale, but my father is Raven. We always follow our mother's clan, so all my siblings are Killerwhale. It's the only aquatic clan."

Like many kids, James represents a mix of cultures. He's Tsimshian, Tlingit, Mexican, Irish, and Italian, but he identifies with his Tsimshian culture the most because it was inherited through his mother. That and because he's from Metlakatla, population 1,400, where you must be part of a Tsimshian family to live on this federal reserve.

"I am related to most of the island," James jokes. This is the most southern community in Alaska, but it's only been here since 1887, when an Anglican Englishman named Reverend William Duncan led 823 Canadian Tsimshian over the border to the Territory of Alaska because he wanted more freedom to worship than he had had in Canada. Before he built on Annette Island, Duncan asked for permission from a Tlingit chief, and then he traveled all the way to Washington, D.C., to get permission from U.S. President Grover Cleveland!

James attends Charles R. Leask Sr. Middle School, where he is one of eighteen seventh-graders. He enjoys Native art class, language arts, shop, wrestling, cross-country, and working as the radio tech during basketball games. He rides his bike or skateboards in summers. In winters, there's hardly any snow, so he loves to get around on his three-wheeled Sole Skates.

James is the youngest of six kids. With the death of their single mother, Mary Florence Gue, their eldest sister became the guardian of her siblings. Rebecca Gue is respected for modeling Tsimshian ways of

Facing: The symbol of the Killerwhale Clan graces James's regalia. Behind him is his village of Metlakatla, reachable only by plane or boat. Above, left: James and his sisters, including two sets of twins, are a family bound together by the eldest, Rebecca Gue, in blue. Symbols of Killerwhale adorn each drum and the bentwood box that James holds. Right: James and his best friend strike a pose by a totem pole at their school.

Above, left: Metlakatla's long house faces the ocean with a richly painted screen of Tsimshian images. Right: Geologists date the unique rocks of Annette Island's Yellow Hill to the Cretaceous Period, more than 66 million years ago.

living for the kids. Aiding her are mentors—an aunt and, as tradition dictates, the uncles of their Killerwhale clan.

In a family photo of the siblings, James has orange hair, but today it's blue. That and his electric red pants offer splashes of color on an otherwise gray day, when the steely saltwater seems to merge with mountain mist and sky. Even the brightly painted long house seems muted as James climbs the deck railings, stretching out his long legs.

"I've had red, orange, pink, and yellow hair," James says, smiling. "For me, it really depends on what holiday is coming up."

How different from the grim-faced black-and-white photos of his ancestors. Perhaps because their lives were harder. Back in Canada, Reverend Duncan declared their Native beliefs and practices unholy and unwelcome. They abandoned their Tsimshian culture and their homeland to create a new home in a

faraway forest. They built a town hall, school, store, and a salmon cannery; they built boardwalks over stumpy ground to connect homes. They posed for formal photos, looking very English in nineteenth-century stiff collars, suits, and dresses.

"The people agreed not to potlatch, dance, sing," says Rebecca, James's sister. "They had to leave that all behind. So when they came here, they did give it up, but they were doing singing, dancing, potlatching in secrecy." One man who saw no evil in the old ways was Sidney Campbell. Like James and his siblings, he was from the Killerwhale clan. Through the early 1900s, as he was serving as a church leader, Campbell also secretly carved, made regalia, drummed, and danced with other Tsimshian people.

James likewise finds no conflicts between his life as a Tsimshian and a Christian. He and his friends attend more than one church youth group. At Metlakatla Presbyterian Church, a framed newspaper photo features James and other local dancers.

"I've only been dancing for three years," James says, "but I do love expressing my culture and who I am." Several Native dance groups are active around town, including Ts'maay ("Ancestors"), Git Leeksa Aks ("People of the Rising Tide"), and Git Susit'aama ("People of a New Beginning").

Near the dancers' photo is a framed proclamation from the church's state leadership. Written in October 1991, it's an apology to all Alaska Natives: " . . . we disavow those teachings which led people to believe that abandoning Native culture was a prerequisite for being Christian."

In the six decades after Reverend Duncan died, more and more Tsimshian were leaning toward their Tsimshian ways and language. In the early 1980s, artist David Albert Boxley helped his people in their journey, reaching out to Canadian relatives for advice. In 1986, Metlakatla hosted its first potlatch, a celebratory feast with Native singing, dancing, drumming, and storytelling. The people reclaimed some of what was lost.

Back home, James's teenaged sister is nested in a chair, her lap covered with yards of red-and-black material. She is adding buttons to a Killerwhale robe. Displayed among family photos are other handmade regalia pieces, including an exquisitely carved Killerwhale headpiece, which is worn at potlatches.

"We're lucky because this is all we've known. We were raised in it," Rebecca says. "But for them [older cousins], it was a totally new thing. We're taking what we know and using it, but we're ever evolving, creating new traditions while we're at it. We're still learning." James flips through his Native art sketchbooks.

James is already showing great skill in Tsimshian art and looks forward to carving wooden masks, boxes, and totems someday.

He's been practicing the distinctive shapes of Tsimshian artistry: the boxy eyes, sweeping wings, fins, claws, beaks, and ears of the creatures his ancestors have illustrated for centuries. They can be seen on totem poles all over this town and in the regalia at potlatches that stretch over four days.

"I finished up S designs, and I have to do N box designs next," James says, comparing the softer lines of wings to the hard edges around eyes. "Then I have to do animal heads, which would be Eagle, Raven, Wolf, and Killerwhale." He can't wait to move on to carving wood. They'll begin with a spoon and go on to bigger pieces, eventually to totem-carving. His teacher is impressed by how fast James is advancing.

"He asked me how I do what I do. I tell him it's in my blood, in my genes, because a lot of my family has done Native art," James says. "We all love to embrace our culture."

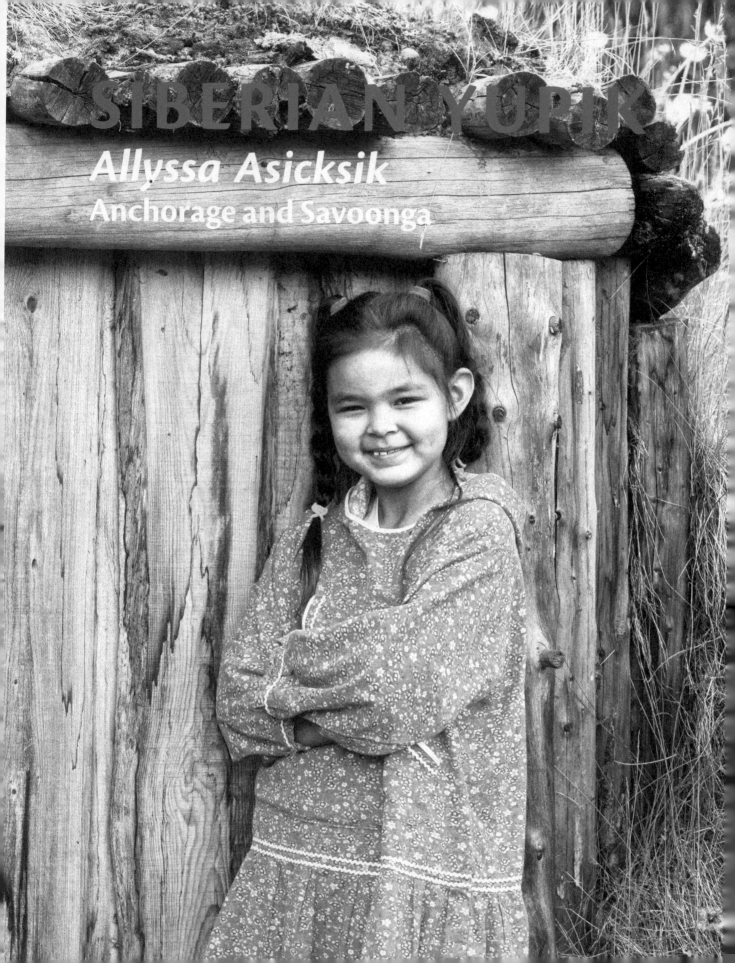

SIBERIAN YUPIK

Allyssa Asicksik
Anchorage and Savoonga

When Allyssa Asicksik says she's going home, she might be talking about Anchorage, Alaska's biggest city, where she has a bedroom in two different houses. There's one at her mom and stepdad's house and another at her dad and stepmom's house. Then again, Allyssa might be talking about her *other* home, Savoonga [suh-VOON-guh], population 800. It's one of only two Siberian Yupik communities remaining on St. Lawrence Island, far from Anchorage, way out in the Bering Sea.

"I would describe it as small, not big," the fourth-grader says simply. Allyssa doesn't go into detail about how her island is closer to Russia—just 35 miles away—than mainland Alaska. Or that St. Lawrence Island is home to the most talented fossil ivory carvers in the world, including her big brothers. They dig up the tusks and bones of long-dead marine mammals and create amazing art for galleries. Or how generations of her family have been reindeer herders. Even now.

Home "here" and home "there" are 700 miles apart, and each marks a special piece of Allyssa's identity. She has family and friends in both places, and either location is great for her favorite nine-year-old activities: making Slime, baking cookies and cupcakes, building forts in the living room, and hosting sleepovers.

"Me and my friends usually go to sleep at two o'clock in the morning," Allyssa says with a smile. "One time we had five girls."

Each year, Allyssa's family makes several trips to their island, where a wide network of loved ones welcomes them. There's freedom in a place you can "play out," as Allyssa calls it, where you can roam and play snowy games while grown-ups quietly keep watch.

"I can yell as much as I want," Allyssa says, "and walk all over. I made my own slide. But I don't go on my butt, I go on my feet, with my boots."

This summer, she's looking forward to riding four-wheelers (which are all called "Hondas") to explore an inland waterfall she's never seen. Her island is treeless and rocky, and while it may look barren to an outsider, the sky, sea, and land are very much alive. For thousands of years, Siberian Yupiks have survived on marine mammals and birds, reindeer meat, and

Facing: In Anchorage, Allyssa loves to explore the Alaska Native Heritage Center, where life-sized replicas of traditional Native homes teach visitors about various cultures. Above, left: Inside a model sod home, Allyssa's mom, Yaari Toolie, explains how a simple stone lamp could light and warm a small space. Right: Using a sharp ulaaq, Allyssa's Aunt Laurie cuts bite-sized pieces of mangtak, bowhead whale skin and blubber, a favorite food.

Above, left: Anchorage is as much like St. Lawrence Island as moose are like baby seals. Still, as different as they are, the two hometowns are just right for Allyssa. Right: Back on the island, her family includes skilled ivory carvers and a long line of reindeer herders.

tundra harvests. The weather is infamous—sometimes delivering sideways snow that can ground the small planes traveling to and from the nearest mainland city of Nome. Other times the sky is so sunny and bright that you can't see without sunglasses or goggles. The people all know each other and look forward to dancing, drumming, singing, and eating together.

Allyssa's favorite Native food is bowhead whale mangtak [MUNG-tuk], the skin and blubber. Her face lights up when she hears the word. Even Allyssa's kitty shares her love of Native food, especially walrus and mangtak. The kitty's name perfectly reflects her cravings: Neqepik, which means "traditional foods." When Neqepik hears Allyssa's mother cutting meat with her ulaaq [OO-lock] knife, the cat comes running.

Allyssa's other home, Anchorage, with its diverse population of nearly 300,000, is sometimes called "Alaska's biggest Native village." More Alaska Natives

live in Anchorage than in all the rest of the state. Natives move there for jobs, for travel and shopping, or for access to medical care. And although they are far from home, the St. Lawrence Island people living in Anchorage bring along their favorite traditions and foods.

Allyssa's mom, Yaari Toolie, moved to the city so long ago that she's gotten used to its size. Still, Yaari wanted to make sure that her kids didn't lose connection with their culture. So Allyssa attends the Alaska Native Culture Charter School, and her Anchorage home regularly hosts St. Lawrence people for banquets of walrus, mangtak, fry bread, and more.

"Remember how we do in our culture?" Yaari asks Allyssa. Together, they recall the hours it takes to prepare for their guests. All the meat must be cut into bite-sized pieces in advance.

"You sit on the floor with cardboard and ulaaq," Allyssa explains. "We cut [the meat] and we put it in piles on trays." During a feast, Allyssa helps carry trays to serve, first elders, then adults, and finally, the youngest.

This summer, Allyssa is spending time with her mom at the Alaska Native Heritage Center in Anchorage, where Yaari works sharing the St. Lawrence Island Yupik culture with busloads of tourists. Visitors wandering through the ANHC and its outdoor displays often ask Yaari about the beautiful tattoos on her face and arms. St. Lawrence Island women wore chin tattoos for centuries, but the custom faded away. "I was scared, but I had to do it," Yaari says. Even Allyssa was ready to join the ancient tradition when she was tiny.

"She mimicked me when she was about two years old," Yaari says with a laugh. "I saw she had used a marker to mark herself." Sitting nearby, Allyssa smiles, even though she doesn't remember.

Traditions of St. Lawrence Island include membership in a clan. Allyssa is a member of the Aymaaramka [uh-MAR-um-guh] clan, which means "strong people." Unlike those in the Southeast Alaska moieties, their clans do not include animal crests, and membership is handed down through the fathers instead of the mothers.

Allyssa's grandmother's clan is Qiwwaghmii [key-WAH-a-mee], or "people of the other side." That's the other side of the Bering Strait—in Siberia, Russia—where relatives have lived for centuries and still do. They share many customs and understand each other's language. At least once a year, the families on each side get to visit.

"At one point we lost contact with them for over fifty years," Yaari says, remembering when eastern Russia was part of the Soviet Union, and Americans

were not allowed to enter. With government changes in 1989, the Siberian Yupiks on each side of the Bering Strait saw each other again for the first time.

"What was great was that these people knew what clan they belonged to, so that's how we located our lost families," Yaari says.

Allyssa has six big brothers, all of them much older than she. Her parents had hoped for more children. Finally they got their wish when she was born to other family members on the island, and they happily adopted her. Along with her Siberian Yupik birth, Allyssa is truly a mixing bowl of cultures. Her stepfather is African American and Apache Indian. Her birth grandfather was a Tlingit baby adopted by a Siberian Yupik couple. Now she is learning about her stepmother's Native culture: twice a week, Allyssa practices Tsimshian dancing in Anchorage.

Whatever the location, whatever the culture, as long as Allyssa is with the people she loves, she will always be at home.

Allyssa's mother decided to tattoo her chin in the same way St. Lawrence Island women have done for centuries. Her body art leads friendly tourists to ask about her culture.

GLOSSARY

IÑUPIAT [en-NEW-pee-at] The People

Aana [AH-nuh] Grandmother

Aqutuq [uh-qoo-tooq] Eskimo ice cream, made from whipping animal fat and berries; sometimes shredded meat or boiled fish flakes are added

Iñupiaq [en-NEW-pee-ack] An individual, the culture, or the language of Alaska's northernmost people

Muktuk [MUCK-tuck] Whale skin and blubber, usually eaten raw or frozen

Uġruk [OO-gruck] Bearded seal

EYAK [EE-yack] People, or Human Beings

Eyak Now-extinct language of the Eyak people. The last Native speaker, Marie Jones, died in 2008.

YUP'IK [YOU-pick] Real Person

Cup'ik [CHOO-pick] A dialect of the Yup'ik language

Manaqing [mahn-OCK-ing] Ice fishing

Ulaq [OO-lock] Curved knife, sometimes called "ulu"

Yugtun [YOUX-toon] Language of Yup'ik people

HAIDA [HI-duh] People

Haida Ancestral language of the Haida people

Haida Gwaii [HI-duh GWHY] Islands of the People, formerly known as the Queen Charlotte Islands of British Columbia, Canada; also the name for Haidas who reside there

Kaigani Haida [kigh-GONE-ee HI-duh] Alaskan Haida whose ancestors migrated from Haida Gwaii

ATHABASCAN [ath-uh-BASK-un] People

Gwich'in [GWITCH-un] "People of the Caribou"; also one of eleven distinct Athabascan languages within Alaska's Interior

UNANGAX̂ [ooh-NAHN-gach] Person

Aleut [al-ee-OOT] Another name for a person from the Unangax̂ culture

Atlatl [AT-ul-AT-ul] Carved wood "throwing stick" used to increase the speed and accuracy of spears

Barabara [buh-RA-buh-RA] Semi-subterranean traditional home with driftwood supporting the walls and ceiling

Qungaayux̂ [COO-nay-ach] Pink salmon, or "humpies"

Slavonic Language of songs and worship in Russian Orthodox Church

Unangam Tunuu Language of the Unangax̂ (Aleut)

TLINGIT [KLINK-it] People of the Tides

Hoonah clans

　Chookaneidí [Chew-cun-ay-DEE]

　T'akdeintaan [Duck-dane-tawn]

　Wooshkeetaan [Woosh-key-tawn]

　Kaagwaantaan [Cog-wahn-tawn]

I likoodzí [Eee-tla-COOT-zee] "You are awesome (or amazing, wonderful)."

Ix̂six̂án [Eex-si-xon] "I love you."

Kooxwuduya [Koox-woo-doo-yuh] "Something brought back to its place of origin."

Xunaa Shuká Hít Ancestors' House

Xunaa Protected from the North Wind, the tribal name for the village of Hoonah

ALUTIIQ [Uh-LOO-tick] True Person

Chenega [chuh-NEE-guh] "Beneath the Mountain"

Chenega Bay One of many communities within the Chugach region

Sugt'stun [SOOK-stoon] Language of Alutiiq people

Sugpiaq [SUG-pea-ak] Another tribal name for the Alutiiq people

TSIMSHIAN [sim-she-ANN] Inside the Skeena River (ancestral homeland in Canada)

Git Leeksa Aks [Git lay-icksha aksh] "People of the Rising Tide," a dance group's name

Git Susit'aama [git sue-sit-am-mah] "People of a New Beginning," a dance group's name

Sm'algvax [Sim-al-gyuck] Language of the Tsimshian, meaning "true language"

Ts'maay [tsim-may] "Ancestors," a dance group's name

Ts'msyen [tsim-sean] Tribal name for Tsimshian

SIBERIAN YUPIK People

Apa [Ah-pa] Grandfather

Aymaaramka [uh-MAR-um-guh] Clan name for "Strong People"

Mangtak [MUNG-tuk] Skin and blubber of whale, usually eaten raw or frozen

Ulaaq [OO-lock] Curved cutting tool (Don't say "ulu." In this language, it means "tongue"—which can also be a cutting tool.)

Qiwwaghmii [key-WAH-a-mee] Clan name for "People of the Other Side"

St. Lawrence Island Yupik Language of Alaska's Siberian Yupik people

OTHER TERMS:

Clan In Tlingit, Haida, and Tsimshian cultures, clans or clan houses are identified by the crest of an animal, fish, bird, reptile, or insect. Membership is passed from mother to child. It's different in the Siberian Yupik culture, where clans are identified by a descriptive name, and membership is passed through fathers. These clans do not claim a crest such as those in southeastern Alaska.

Moiety The first division of a people group that identifies each member's place in society. In the Tlingit culture, people are born into the Eagle or Raven/Wolf moieties, depending on which moiety their mothers are from. Likewise, through their mothers, the Haida people are born either Raven or Eagle. The Tsimshian people also inherit their kinship from their mothers, dividing into one of four phratries (similar to moieties): Killerwhale (Blackfish), Wolf, Raven, and Eagle. Strict social rules define roles for each moiety, from taking care of each other, to training children, to hosting potlatches, to dividing wealth.

Potlatch Cultural gatherings with well-defined rules and with varied functions. In southeastern cultures, they are feasts which include gift-giving, stories, adoptions into clans, memorials, dancing and drumming, and an overall celebratory time to express tribal pride. In the Athabascan culture, they are area gatherings with deep historical ties. Depending on the community, they may include storytelling, old-time fiddling and jig dancing, waltzes, or traditional tribal dances. Again, sharing food is a central part of the celebration. In the Gwich'in Athabascan region, the word is pronounced POT-lotch; in Southeast, it's POT-latch.

Regalia Ceremonial clothing and objects unique to each culture. Tlingit, Haida, and Tsimshian people wear their formal regalia during the Juneau dance gathering called Celebration, as well as for local potlatches recognizing totem pole-raisings, memorials, weddings, and other joyous occasions. Athabascan, Unangax̂, Yup'ik, Alutiiq, Eyak, Siberian Yupik, and Iñupiat people each wear their culture's unique clothes, headgear, gloves, and/or footwear when they come together for special dances and other occasions.

Tricia Brown has written and edited dozens of books since she first made Alaska her home in 1978. In a career that evolved from newspapers to magazines to book publishing, her writing is inspired by Alaska, reflected in nearly thirty titles on Native cultures, dog mushing, Last Frontier living, reference, and travel. Among Tricia's ten children's books are reader favorites, such as *The Itchy Little Musk Ox*, *Groucho's Eyebrows*, and *Charlie and the Blanket Toss*. She travels often for school and library visits, where she urges students to water the creative seeds inside of them. Tricia and her husband Perry make their home in Anchorage with their granddaughter, Kierra, and a naughty-but-darling golden retriever named Willow. See www.triciabrownbooks.com.

As one of Alaska's accomplished photojournalists, **Roy Corral** has traveled extensively throughout the Far North's remote regions photographing and writing about remarkable people and places for more than three decades. His photographic images have appeared in *National Geographic* and *Forbes*, and are also on display at the Smithsonian Arctic Studies Center, Anchorage Museum, and the Alaska Native Heritage Center. Roy is the former photo editor of *Alaska*, and his stories were published in *Alaska* and *First Alaskans* magazines. His collaborative book projects include *Alaska Native Ways*, *My Denali*, *A Child's Glacier Bay*, *Children of the Midnight Sun*, and *Chugach: Reflections of the People, Land and Sea*. Roy calls Eagle River, Alaska, home.

Facing: In winter, the sun is just a ball of color in the sky and offers little warmth.

Back cover, left, from top: Leah Moss, Ethan Sparck, Cyanna Bereskin, Hunter McCarty, and Aaliyah Tiedeman. Right, from top: Allyssa Asicksik, Tyler Kramer, Alyson Seville, James Williams, and Juuyāay Christianson.

Praise for *Children of the Midnight Sun*:

"*Children of the Midnight Sun* acknowledges the drastic changes of the last few decades, with the advent of satellite television, access to transportation, and the Internet, but focuses on the preservation or reawakening of culture through each child." —*Kirkus Reviews*

"Author and artist successfully communicate the common thread linking these eight lives: the importance of Native traditions, family bonds and the wisdom and experience of preceding generations as they navigate in modern times." —*Publishers Weekly*

"For Native children, growing up in Alaska today means dwelling in a place where traditional practices sometimes mix oddly with modern conveniences. *Children of the Midnight Sun* explores the lives of eight Alaskan Native children, each representing a unique and ancient culture. This extraordinary book also looks at the critical role elders play in teaching the young Native traditions." —Children's Book Council

"Brown seems to have anticipated the kinds of things kids would want to ask about these Alaskans, given the chance, and offers readers a glimpse at eight distinct personalities and ways of life. . . . All who read *Children of the Midnight Sun* will come away with an enriched view of the lives of young native Alaskans." —*School Library Journal*

"The violet-and-crimson photo of a sunset on the jacket immediately dispels the narrow image of Alaska as a stark, uninviting place. Inside are more excellent photos, all taken by Roy Corral, which show Alaska's vibrant contrasts—snow-swept villages and manicured city gardens, native dances and trips to the mall." —Booklist

CPSIA information can be obtained
at www.ICGtesting.com
Printed in the USA
BVHW010207040721
611096BV00002B/2